RUNNERS

Gerald Hausman

RUNNERS

Sunstone Press
Santa Fe, New Mexico

ACKNOWLEDGEMENTS

To the following publications, I am most grateful for first publication of the poems in this collection: *Arizona Quarterly, Ararat, New Mexico Wildlife, The Christian Science Monitor, Cafe Solo, Snowy Egret, The Third Berkshire Anthology, Bloomsbury Review, Grasshopper #1, Country Journal, Southwestern Review, Longhouse, Anthology of Magazine Verse, Yearbook of American Poetry, 1984* and *Oyez Review.*

FIRST EDITION
Printed in the United States of America

Library of Congress Cataloging in Publication Data:

Hausman, Gerald A., 1945-
    Runners.

    I. Title.
PS3558.A76R8   1984   811'.54   84-2487

ISBN: 0-86534-052-8 hard cover
      0-86534-022-6 paperback

Published in 1984 by Sunstone Press / Post Office Box 2321 / Santa Fe, NM 87504-2321 / USA

"...I will bring thy seed from the east, and gather
thee from the west; I will say to the north, give up;
and to the south, keep not back..."

ISAIAH

CONTENTS

PART I: SEEDING FROM THE EAST

9 / The Parsley Garden
10 / The Black Widow Webbing
11 / Diane Wakoski in the Bird Sanctuary
12 / Dylan Thomas at the White Horse
13 / Winfield Townley Scott
14 / The Last Time I Saw Aunt Glad
16 / Ten Mile Woods in Winter
17 / Wood for Winter
17 / The Eel Falls

PART II: GATHERING FROM THE WEST

19 / Runners
20 / Three Houses and the Word I
22 / No Moon Night
22 / Aspens
22 / Ravens
23 / Song on the Road to Chimayo
23 / Tanque Verde
24 / Dunton
26 / Pueblo Water

PART III: SAYING TO THE NORTH

29 / Elk Bone Promises
30 / The Fallen
31 / Autumn in the Mountains
32 / Heron and Trout, The Air We Breathe
33 / Angel Fire
34 / Ending Up in Horse Creek Canyon After Being Lost for Hours
35 / Letters from the Rio Grande Gorge, at Dusk,
      During Three Winter Crossings

PART IV: KEEPING TO THE SOUTH

38 / Red Roads, Leafy Rivers
39 / Survivors of Singing River
40 / Goat Castle, Natchez
42 / The Great Salamander Migration of Seventy-Five
43 / Porches
44 / Witnesses
45 / Portrait of a Man in a Pink Shirt Under Coconut Palms
46 / Six Decorations on a Mexican Beach
47 / Island Dreams

PART I:

SEEDING FROM THE EAST

THE PARSLEY GARDEN
for William Saroyan

He kept them by his cash register
and his cot, great loads of round
river-bottom stones.

By his own admission, he had become
some kind of Sisyphus
rolling them up hills
he had no business
trying to scale.

And he lamented the passing
of the passenger pigeon,
the disappearance of the Great Northern
where he cranked out words
that won him a Pulitzer he refused.

He once said he liked what I did
at a time when I lived
off comments other writers made
about my work.

Now I have my own dead river bed
of sun-dappled stones to consider,
my own passenger pigeons,
and Saroyan no longer strolls the streets
of Paris shaping those words
which were the last parsley garden
in American letters.

THE BLACK WIDOW WEBBING
for Eliot Porter

"One morning," he said, "the net was everywhere,
and on each circuit of filament,
a newborn spider."

I saw that misty morning web
filling the studio
like the topsail of a ghost ship.

"What did you do," I asked.

"Left the front door open and every last one
was gone by nightfall... think of all those spiderlings
filling the universe outside my door."

After that I wondered when I looked at studios
and barns and well-covers and window casements
and for a while I thought the world
was one great sultry hairnet fanning-out
in all directions, wherever I looked
wherever I went—

one vast desert weaving of deadly storytelling.

DIANE WAKOSKI IN THE BIRD SANCTUARY

We had come up the
        mountain road
under the dripping elms
to that place
        in the bird sanctuary
where the reservoir
        lay in a fog
        of stars
and she said, that poet of piece-
meals, that blood factory
        of feelings—

What are those harsh-sounding
croaking things, frogs?

No, I said, fogs.

Are you sure?

Let's take off our cloaks
and dive into their croaks.

I'm going back to the car,
she said,
and did.

DYLAN THOMAS AT THE WHITE HORSE

Halsey said – and I'm sure it was so
that Dylan's face
     resembled the underbelly
     of an octopus.
The seashore image fits
     more ways than one:
the night he passed out
     in a seawell
     of his own puke.
"Pleasure," the bartender said
     Irishly to Halsey –
"to mop up after the greatest
     lyric poet
of the twentieth century..."
     whereupon
     he raised head
     by curly hair
of Welsh gab-street potted-poet
and wiped clean the boozy bay
     he'd fish-fallen-into.

WINFIELD TOWNLEY SCOTT

I watch the stilted heron poke
its bamboo beak
into the dusky water
and suddenly remember
what he said –
"Write. Keep writing."

When I'd promised myself
to quit, go straight,
this was a hard line.
But it kept me taut,
and taught.

Then he died of a fashionable
overdose and his wife Ellie
was killed by a car driven
by her son.

Tonight, I see one of his
favorite images
stuck to an oily piling
in the bay – a snail
working its poem-slow way
a slippery trail
that says, in silver,
what no one knows
or cares to remember
this wet salt October night:
he was here.

THE LAST TIME I SAW AUNT GLAD

I took her to a wedding
in ninety degree august heat.
Her shoes too tight,
I boosted her heavy body
in and out
of the car.
Afterwards,
she asked for a pint
coffee ice cream
she ate beside
me on the porch.

"Under those birch trees,
you boxed Charlie Reed,
the doctor's son.
You beat him fair and square,
made your dad proud.
Think I'll
go upstairs now."

One foot at a time.
I raised the right,
she raised the left.
We made it to the open window
with the fan and the chair
where she could listen
to the afternoon bells,
completely
out of breath, dazed
by the heat.

"Can't be anything too serious,
I sleep too good nights."
I left her sitting by the window,
looking down at the bare spot
under the pines
where I once buried
a box of bottle caps
Charlie Reed
never found.

TEN MILE WOODS IN WINTER

The woods no longer cricket thick,
snow fog off birch banks.
I come back to the place
where our bodies
sank out of sight
in summer fern.
Our clothes, a white island
in a night that whistled
with toads.
Now, on the frozen pond,
I recognize the fins of carp –
they glide like hands
on bodies wet with sweat and dew.

WOOD FOR WINTER

Spiders spin
sacs
that swing
in the
wind.

Foxes bark
at the
cold.

Grasshoppers
on stiff
legs
sing
a scapegrace
song.

I have
not
cut
enough
wood.

THE EEL FALLS

Living in the silver lining
of the falls –
black cunning life
shiny ribbon with teeth;
eyes more bird
than fish.

When it died from a clever
hook, the fisherman said –
''– mighty good eating
them things –''
black smoke in the sun,
the falls thus fallen
once and for all.

Who among us, then,
would send a smooth
skipping-stone
into the silver lining,
hoping to trick out
that dark spool of death?

PART II:

GATHERING FROM THE WEST

RUNNERS

The oldest dance on earth
begins and ends
with the heart.
No saying can enter
the sun wind, the hawk look
the coyote foot, the ancestral
heart forever harking back.

I run on the coiled-clay shards
of those who were once
formed by sun, cloud, sand –
who came out of the earth
without logic.

I run on the
shapely bones
of those who
were once like us, the runners,
with feet of dust, who
begin and end
with the heart
and its singular saying
forever
harking back
without logic
to the oldest dance on earth.

THREE HOUSES AND THE WORD I

pine house / one

I once dreamt I would live
in a simple cabin
surrounded by sleeping fir trees.
Now, fifteen years later
that cabin built, lived in,
left. My eldest girl spoke
her first syllables there.
When it rained, the upstairs
windows open, taste of moist bark
on the tongue all day long.

mud house / two

I said when I moved to the desert,
I would die here, liking
clean stone better than leprous
lichen. My house in the sand hills
a sunlit jar, the front yard,
no yard, a delectable waste
of gleaming bones. I suppose
one day, as my friend said, I'll end up
"...a collection of wrinkles
in a cactus garden,
a crow sawing away at my shoulder."

sky house / three

The last house made of wind, made of dawn.
I will live there after
the other two
have fallen down
and the word for shelter
is the word for I;
the house of wind and dawn
lived in by nobody I know.

NO MOON NIGHT

How does
one November
cricket
make it

if pine wind
says
hush
to even
the loudest
stars

ASPENS

Aspen leaves
in autumn rain
stop moving
a minute
stop reasoning
with the sun –
go down on brown
this dark thursday,
stay golden
a little longer,
a lot stiller.

RAVENS

We hear them saw-cough
as we sit
on the headland hill
among sheep dip
and cattle dung.

They cuddle the clouds
high over Eagle Nest.

Six hundred feet below
wind riffles
green feathers
of the lake.

Naked, we own all
but our own skin.

SONG ON THE ROAD TO CHIMAYO

Black winter clouds bunch over Sangres,
low hills, pinon-squat, juniper-bent,
vacant life.

I watch storm move down mountains,
undertaker ravens dine on carcass
of dog.

We will all be divied-up one day –
white crows, black snow
down the road to Chimayo.

TANQUE VERDE

You said, I remembered:
"impolite to talk
when wind burns
and saguaros dance" –

sitting, two of us
high over desert floor
looking down on level
plain where mule deer
browse among thorns.

DUNTON

Rest easy, the ghosts seem to say,
nothing to do here
now the silver's gone.
All night the waterfall
out our window
files its silver claim,
glittery foil on moss green stone.

A she-bear wanders across the meadow
full of mountain gentian
startling the town burro
into a bawling chorus
of hees and haws.

Nothing else happens.
I wonder in the dark
what happened to the years –

In the distance
honkytonkers live-out
the last hours
of the broken down bar
above the river.
No one but the bear
believes they exist.

I get up in the sleeping cabin
to watch a woman, half naked
the other side of the road
waltzing in a pink shirt
by a flickering fire.

Her family is sound asleep –
like mine. Alarmed, she
stops the articulate curves
of her dance; looks out
into the waterfall night.
The roar of applause
follows her every move.

Someone, in one of the sleeping
cabins, reaches under her shirt.

PUEBLO WATER

1   The stream's
not so pure anymore.
Boys
throw stones at the old One
who stoops with plastic pail
as they aim and fire, hoping
to catch him off-balance,
watch him fall.

2   Ladders going up lean
in crazy angles, throw dizzy
shadows at girls
with new breasts, running
like American children anywhere,
doors slamming when they get
there; still the old One
with the stroke-afflicted arm
doesn't fall. Stones
spank the stream near his third
bucket of water.
The small boy who throws
lies down on the mud brown
bank, curls up in pretend-sleep,
watched over by big shouldered
gaunt-furred wolf dog with
slant blue eyes.

3   Bell chimes in the church square.
Smoke speaks in the many
chimneyed homes
of mud.

Smaller than pictures,
browner, more desolate, more
humble; shadows it
casts the same clean lines
that caught the red-bearded
Englishman
who fed Taos and Taormina
into the water of literature.

4   Sundown. We have not moved.
Car with Navajo Nation
Symbol on door pulls up.
Two girls with flat moonfaces
survey the mud
order of simple squares
their great-grandfathers plundered
for silver, blankets, meat
and women.

In the safety of their car,
they laugh.

The old One on the slippery bank
does not fall, his fourth bucket
of pueblo water
grabs up the moon.

PART III:

SAYING TO THE NORTH

ELK BONE PROMISES

Wind in aspen –
the old metaphysical burden
of constancy in love
fall away,
nine thousand vertical feet.

Down the elk track rock trail
heard, just now, the sagey warbler –
mountain thrasher, Phil called it.

Above Red River
up a talus slope
sitting at sundown
watching worms
make silken lifelines.

My own lifelines drift
down hill,
taken by the silk wind.

"You did right," he said
"burning those early poems."

On the way back
I find an elk bone
blasted from another life,
another time. Handing it to him, I say:

"Here is a promise
I will not burn."

THE FALLEN

You stare at that bare
snow-scar
over timberline
When sun hits
wet aspens
noon of mountain rain,
you see snow
even in summer.

We didn't know –
looking on –
but the snow
made august and aspens
all the more
quivering and constant
in summer-killing
green.

What he didn't count on,
the one who fell, was this
change of weather.

One way to go –
hang on a pinnacle
nine hours in a snowstorm
twelve thousand feet up
while a copter hovers
like a dragonfly caught
in a cloud.

As he watched and waited,
he died. The copter
came into the sun,
made a metallic smile
in the blue freeze.

AUTUMN IN THE MOUNTAINS

In a few days, Frank Waters
will leave for Lima. Overhead,
late autumn sun
Wheeler Peak lost in cloud.
I can see the bald part
stretched like elk hide,
heavily salted with snow.
Halloween, they tell me –
otherwise I wouldn't know.
The face of Frank Waters
is mask, not scary but hidden
nonetheless. He is the last
of those early first. And now
he is heading for Peru.
In a place of sun
a man whose name is
water is worthwhile.
I am not wasting anybody's
time saying a pebble,
a feather, a shard are parallel
lines to something we cannot see.
Maybe Frank will tell us
what I mean when he comes
back. I, too, would wear a mask
sit in the plaza watching
the drought of human value
ebb and flow, or go to Peru,
and listen to the wind.
Halloween, autumn in the
mountains, time to wear a mask.

HERON AND TROUT, THE AIR WE BREATHE

Now the deer come down
to drink and browse
in the catclaw acacia.
Desert holly glistens
by the swollen December river.

Suddenly a blue heron
busts out of a winter thicket,
flies big-winged by us in the rain.
His blue body dark
against the bleached sycamore trunks.

I look into the yellow current
and see the little trout
imitate the shadow movement
of the great bird, now gone.

Wind wrinkles the pool;
I watch, content
as trout breathe water-air
the deer and I drink.

ANGEL FIRE

Hiking up white mountain town
steeples and spires, iron ski lift chairs
musically conversing, clanging
ten thousand feet, all the furry
townsmen gone to sleep but us – we two
firewater in our bellies
crunching up the nightworld chillies.

What did we say, anything that mattered?
I remember your face hidden in a hundred scarves,
the head of a warm-muffled worm.
My feet – a couple of black tongues
clumping out words
in the dark ups and downs –
Thus it was
a worm and a couple of random tongues
hiked halfway up to midnight –
sleep camp of the fallen angels.

**ENDING UP
IN
HORSE CREEK
CANYON
AFTER
BEING LOST
FOR HOURS**

The arroyo a funnel for ghosts –
flotsam of pine, spillway of bone.
Bending down I see white awful
wreckage of skeleton horse,
as if – standing whole –
the horse had been bowled by a giant,
and broken into shards.
For a mile up canyon I count them,
each piece a sand-burnished treasure.
The fluted neck bone, swanlike and
firm, stuck in a calcite bed,
mica shining all around it.
The romantic in me says once
this horse stood proud,
mane to the wind, moon
in its eye. Quickly
I remember minnows eating out
my hand the day I dumped
my father's ashes from a copper
urn into a sunlit lake.
Better to have been a horse
than a man, I think – wrong or not –
and to wander a back country canyon
until the time fate should
bowl you down to bits of bone.
I take the jawbone back home
mount it in a window
so those mad teeth can still
bite at the moon,
and remind me of being lost
and found in Horse Creek Canyon.

**LETTERS
FROM THE
RIO GRANDE
GORGE,
AT DUSK,
DURING THREE
WINTER
CROSSINGS**

1   You said the distance, between us,
     was deeper than that hole in the
     earth, that canyon we crossed
     in the snow.
     You said
     we couldn't cross it except at
     night, the flakes
     moth-beating the windshield of our
     jeep, keeping us in hot
     metal-moving tent of zippered
     darkness. Safe, you said it was,
     at sixty, skipping over the gorge.

2   Another time,
     forced to the edge,
     pointed straight off
     switchback of fear.
     We swallowed
     hard, jeep took it,
     abyss calling our names,
     looking down into
     river bottom of the world,
     scarf of white fire-ice.
     Skidding once –
     blue pickup truck too
     close.
     Calling of
     our names
     in syllables of dusk.

3 You said the distance was deeper
   between us afterward.
   I said we came out alive.
   You said we had met the Mountain.
   I said we had been born in the Mountain's belly.
   You said, may I cut your fingernails
   once before we die?
   I said, they've turned into claws.
   You said, the distance was no deeper
   than that hole in the earth,
   that canyon we crossed
   in the snow.

PART IV:

KEEPING TO THE SOUTH

RED ROADS, LEAFY RIVERS

1

Lost in old kudzu vines,
fallen barns
of the south –
grey wood
growing greyer
in mossy night
of magnolia mist.

Cotton's king no more.
Fields lying fallow
at roadside,
weevils beating the delta
blue,
blacks bending to the same
muscle-weary tune.

2

The rivers run
like cottonmouths
under red roads
that go deep
into Georgia
Alabama
Louisiana
Mississippi,
the true south
of kudzu-covered graves
elderly trees,
pain unspoken.

3

Beside the fatherly oaks
the ladies are standing,
blossoms in place,
waiting, in the moss
beguiling,
the red roads
and leafy rivers
endlessly sorrowing.

4

I have come home
to a place
still unborn.
A place of
still-born
days to come.

SURVIVORS OF SINGING RIVER
for Choctaw Jim

In your dreams, did you see the children
float by without eyes, without names.

When the drowning was done, did you dry
yourself off and fade back into the dark
legend of your birth.

Tell us what you felt
when they gathered your tribe –
beads upon a string –
cast them into the center
of Singing River.
A sight to sink beneath our sight;
a death to do death to our dignity.

In your dreams, did you have a child
with eyes of flint whose name
was fire unkilled by water,
or was no-name the name
for offspring never born.

Note: Singing River, the name the Pascagoula Indians of
Mississippi gave to the Pascagoula River, was the site of their
fabled encounter with a warlike neighbor tribe. Rather than
surrender or leave their homeland, they marched with women
and children into the river chanting their death song.
No one has ever explained why they did not fight.

GOAT CASTLE, NATCHEZ

No one wants to talk now
of nobility gone astray,
gone crazy
for poetry and love of goats
this stalking summer night.

Motorcycles and goat placentas
burn equally well in fire
of the kind Natchez has known.

We sleep in separate sweats
in slave quarters from the
seventeenth century.

In my dreams, I see the gentry
guttering out like candles
in the straws of the elegant ruins
of Goat Castle.

It made the Times
the time murder broke
and no Black fit
the bill of spilling blood.

I keep waking up, wondering
if I can tell it aloud: they
were not devils, I say to
the inadmissible darkness,
hunkering with goats
on Queen Anne's Lace
lapping wine and blood and poetry
as the last straws of memory
burned it down for good,
they were not devils of the confederacy
but misbegotten rumors
of hot tight sheets
fitted for Rimbaud scored
with the red half-moon
marks of love, cloven-style.

I wake and sleep, wake and sleep
until dawn
when the grey goes blue again
and I think: if brother went against
brother, then surely a goat for lover
was no cause for murder.

THE GREAT SALAMANDER MIGRATION
OF SEVENTY-FIVE

Once every 12 years – if that –
I was told, but here, now,
in the middle of a trick turn
way past midnight
on the way home
from an already forgotten film,
they are suddenly under the double
burn of my headlights –
piles of wiggling licorice
with prehistoric eyes.
Where are they going,
what is their rush this mad hour?
I see them, armies of yellow-spotted priests,
heading for the swampside of the road.
Admit it: you are afraid to pick one up.
(I am. Hands in pockets, stand and watch,
mute observer.)
"Say me a prayer," I whisper
as they write a riddle
older than bones.
Then I drive home in darkness
and everything is sunspots
on a black ribbon of moving candy.

PORCHES

Now I know the need
for porches,
dry roofs for hard summer rains.

Porches are the place to remember
yesterday's undone thing.
What was it left
unmended, untended,
twenty years too late?

Was it the old plow rusting in the rain?

Pumpkin flowers shoot
into hayrake prongs,
laughing at the loss of memory.

Dry roofs for hard summer rains.

WITNESSES
proverb: love is bees in the stomach

The cactus blossom -
opening at night
closing out
the bees by day.

I don't know
what it was
brought us
to this palo verde plain
of sun and thorn
sugar and salt.

Love, loneliness
wind before rain?

I don't know,
but it is harder
and harder
to board out the bees.

PORTRAIT OF A MAN IN
A PINK SHIRT UNDER COCONUT PALMS

He looks as if nothing would happen to him.
Hibiscus in the air, blue trunks of palms
behind his head.
The sea roars challenge to his posture, one leg
thrown over the turquoise beach chair.
A mango sun hangs in the balance of isle and bay.
The runner with legs like a gazelle
floats by in the dense gathering dusk.
The man in the pink shirt does not move,
nothing can make him shift off center.
An hour past dark he sits, a piece of pink
on a palette of blue palm.

SIX DECORATIONS ON A MEXICAN BEACH

1

In the town square
of Zihuatanejo
it is always noon
unless it is dark
and then it is night.

2

There is a circus in town,
a Mexican circus
with Brazilian lions
that roar when palm
fronds rattle.

3

Trim white yachts
nip and tuck
as harbor waves
roll in and little boys
dive for pennies
the color of their skin.

4

The fruit in the jungle
falls without a sound
and the man who decorates
dinner plates
with banana leaves
listens to the voice
of a fly.

5

There is nowhere
to go when the sun
goes behind Ixtapa
island.

6

Water the color
of a macaw's eye.

ISLAND DREAMS

I dreamt I heard my father's voice
in the white mouth of a shell.

I heard it clearly
on a blue beach by the sea
in the Virgins
where cocoa boys
never heard of snow –

"White flakes fall from sky?"
they sneer, doubting my sanity,
wary of eye and smile
like the squid that comes
upon us in the reef,
purple eyes amazed
in the amazing water
where snow
is no more real
or true
than the speechless voice
of a shell.

ABOUT
THE AUTHOR

Gerald Hausman's devotion to writing began in 1972 as several major anthologies discovered his work in a variety of magazines. During the same period, Hausman founded *The Berkshire Anthology* (now an annual collection featuring prestigious writers from the Berkshires) which in its second issue was funded and distributed through Hirschl & Adler Galleries Inc. in New York City.

His first book, *New Marlboro Stage*, appeared in 1969 (The Bookstore Press) and this was followed, from the same publisher, by *Circle Meadow* in 1972.

Meanwhile more publications and two children's books: *The Boy With The Sun Tree Bow* (Berkshire Traveller Press) in 1973 and *Sitting On The Blue-Eyed Bear: Navajo Myths and Legends* (Lawrence Hill & Co., now from Sunstone Press) in 1975. Then came *The Pancake Book* with his wife, Lorry, in 1976 followed by *The Yogurt Cookbook*, also with his wife, in 1977 (both from Persea Books).

Three new books appeared in 1980: a volume of poems, *Night Herding Song* (Copper Canyon Press); a children's book about whales called *The Day The White Whales Came To Bangor* (Cobblesmith Books); and a mystery novel for adults, *No Witness* (Stackpole).

Hausman's poetry appears frequently in national publications, as well as limited editions.